THE FIFTH SEASON

GALATIANS 6:9

GOD'S PROMISE TO US

#YourSeasonOfRestorationAndAbundance

Jessica,
Thank you !
Dr. Lottie N. Pitts
4/24/22

Lottie N. Pitts

Foreword By
Barbara McCoo Lewis

Inquiries and Book Orders should be addressed to:

Lottie N. Pitts
Email: lottiesgifts1@sbcglobal.net

Great Writers Media
Email: info@greatwritersmedia.com
Phone: 877-600-5469

ISBN: 978-1-957148-74-8 (sc)
ISBN: 978-1-957148-75-5 (ebk)

Rev 3/24/2022

Contents

Acknowledgement

To God be the Glory for the things He has done.

I want to convey my gratitude to my loving husband and pastor, Thaddeus L. Pitts, who always encourages and supports me in all my endeavors.

I also want to thank Mother Barbara McCoo Lewis, the General Supervisor of the International Department of Women, Church Of God In Christ, Inc. who so graciously and willingly accepted the task of writing the foreword for my book. What an honor! Her words of inspiration and wisdom will certainly encourage each reader.

Lastly, I express my love and appreciation to my loving family and Church family for their encouragement and support.

> *"Let not mercy and truth forsake thee: bind them about thy neck; write them upon the table of thine heart: So shalt thou find favour and good understanding in the sight of God and man."* (Proverbs 3:3)

Foreword

Amidst the intensity of life and ministry of Jesus Christ, believers, the followers of Christ, have been given the great commission to spread the gospel, the good news to all nations. But without troubles of this world as Apostle Paul declared in 11 Corinthians 4:8, "We may be troubled on every side, yet not distressed; perplexed, but not in despair; persecuted, but not forsaken; cast down, but not destroyed," as we walk this spiritual journey with Christ by our side.

The author, Dr. Lottie N. Pitts, shares her insight about the vicissitudes and weariness of life, but the saints should be receptive and encouraged by (Galatians 6:9 KJV), "And let us not be weary in well doing: for in due season we shall reap, if we faint not." In essence Apostle Paul is saying, "Don't give up, don't abandon the field in which you have sown, because harvest time will surely come."

Each year we experience the natural four seasons: winter, spring, summer, and fall with each season presenting its own set of benefits and challenges. Dr. Pitts' theme of her book is about the due season known as the fifth season. The word, due, means something that rightfully belongs to you, and season means a special period. When you put them together, we have God saying, "In a special period of time we shall receive the promises and all that rightly belongs to the believer, which she appropriately titled her book, "The Fifth Season: God's Promise to Us."

Dr. Pitts reminds us that we are on God's calendar, and many of us reading this book are on the brink of our fifth season. It may not look like or feel like you are at the breakthrough to the promises of God; but keep striving in the work of the Lord that you have sown in good ground. Your payday is coming, and your deliverance is on the way. It is your season to be blessed.

Our God is a good God, and it is always His intention to bless you despite the circumstances you may be facing. Hard times will bring forth good character when you allow God to perform His perfect will in your life. Submitting to God, you can trust Him to bring you through every trial and circumstances and to "exalt you in due time." (1 Peter 5:6 KJV)

Mother Barbara McCoo Lewis

General Supervisor

International Department of Women

Church Of God In Christ, Inc.

Cover Story

According to Britannica.com, "The cross is the principal symbol of the Christian religion, recalling the Crucifixion of Jesus Christ and the redeeming benefits of his Passion and death. The cross is thus a sign both of Christ himself and of the faith of Christians." Isaiah 53:5 states, *"But he was wounded for our transgressions, he was bruised for our iniquities: the chastisement of our peace was upon him; and with his stripes we are healed."* Child of God, may the cross on the cover remind us of the price Jesus paid on Calvary and its redeeming benefits. Christ died that we might be set free from sin and have everlasting life. With his stripes, we are healed spiritually, emotionally, mentally, and physically. In John 10:10 Jesus declared, *"The thief cometh not, but to steal, and to kill, and to destroy: I am come that they might have life, and that they might have it more abundantly."*

As in the words of the hymn writer, Isaac Watts, it was, "At the cross, at the cross where I first saw the light, and the burden of my heart rolled away. It was there by faith I received my sight, and now I am happy all the day." It was by faith that we accepted Jesus Christ as our personal savior. And now thereafter, our attitude should exhibit a new outlook on life, one that is a positive outlook and not a negative one, one of victory and not defeat, one of great expectation and not disbelief. *"Now faith is the substance of things hoped for, the evidence of things not seen."* (Hebrews 11:1) You don't see it but expect it. By faith, expect a breakthrough to your fifth season, (due season), expect a miracle and an outpouring of God's supernatural favor. My brothers and sisters, your faith will produce the manifestation thereof.

The fifth season in the life of a child of God is their due season if he or she does not faint (grow weak or feeble and give up). It is a season of recovery, restoration, and abundance. It is in this season that the chain of bondage is broken. The chain of lack is broken, and the chain of hurt and shame is broken. Yes, there is power in the name of Jesus to break every chain. For the faithful followers who have called on the name of Jesus for your turn-around season, it is an answer to your prayer and fasting. It is the fulfillment of God's promise to you.

Finally, before you read the first chapter, I want to acknowledge God for the prophecy given to me three years ago declaring "God said you have another book to write." I actually thought my book writing days were over, so I did not give it much thought at all. But how many of you know when it is God's will, your answer should always be, "Yes, Lord."? Because of the Holy Spirit's guidance and inspiration, I completed the draft transcript for this book within months. Based on the anointed text and the reviews and ratings on the first edition so far, He saved the best for last.

I hope and pray that this book will accomplish its primary purpose, which is to emphatically encourage and remind you, a child of

God, that God loves you and your due season is imminent. I pray that this book is the awe-inspiring encouragement and motivation that will generate an indelible impression on your mind and stimulate you to move forward to your next fifth season.

"God is not a man that he should lie; neither the son of man, that he should repent: hath he said, and shall he not do it? Or hath he spoken, and shall he not make it good?" (Numbers 23:19) God, the promise keeper, promised us a due season. So, it's already done in Jesus' name. Therefore, when your due season arrives, you will reap the benefits, and God will get the glory.

The Author

1

Four Natural Seasons

To everything there is a season, and a time
to every purpose under the heaven.

(Ecclesiastes 3:1)

God has set in place a pattern of four natural seasons that occurs each year for us to experience and adapt to. They are spring, summer, fall, and winter. Each season has its own characteristics and is known by its ambiance and climate. Each one tenders both benefits and complexities.

In the Spring warm temperature occurs, and the snowstorms transition into plenty of wind and rain. Wind is moving air. We cannot see it but feel and witness the results of it, which reminds me of the God we serve. We cannot see the Holy Spirit but can feel His mighty power moving and witness the results of His mighty acts. The rain comes and causes the grass to grow, flowers to germinate and blossom, and the trees to bud. It is a time we sow by planting seeds in the dirt and wait in anticipation for the harvest of new flowers, trees, and vegetation to spring forth.

In the Summer there is a lot of sunlight. The days are hot, and the nights are warm. The flowers have blossomed, and the trees are in full bloom. We see the color, green, everywhere. The lawns need cutting and the bushes and hedges trimmed. The gardens are full of flowers or vegetables. Why? Because the Summer Season has arrived and is producing a harvest. The days are longer, and the nights are shorter. Of course, Summer is my favorite season, even though I do not care for the bees, mosquitos, and flies buzzing around. But what can you say? You take the bitter with the sweet.

Summer Harvest

In the Fall the temperature begins to drop. It is cool during the day, and somewhat cold at night. The leaves on the trees begin to change colors. They transition into some of the most beautiful colors you can imagine. The green leaves have now changed to yellow, brown, and orange. Have you ever stopped to admire God's awesome handiwork? It is amazingly picturesque and beautiful to the human eye. However, the colorful leaves do not remain, but fall to the ground. And before you know it, they are now resting all over your beautiful lawn, which now requires the task of raking them. We must remember that the Fall also produces a harvest that the planter (who sows seeds) looks forward to reaping.

Winter has the least amount of sunlight. The temperature drops to freezing and most trees become completely bare, and the pretty flowers have once again faded away. The mowing of the lawn has ceased because the grass has stopped growing or has withered away. The days are shorter, and the nights are longer.

It just does not seem to be enough hours in the day to run errands. You get up in the dark each morning to go to work, and you come home from work in the dark. According to where you reside, you are liable to experience snowstorms, blizzards, sleet, and sub-zero weather during the winter months.

We who live in the Midwest have learned to adapt and endure the winter season each year. However, I do know a few people who really enjoy the winter season. But I must confess that it is one of my least favorite seasons. The good part about Winter is that it does include two of my favorite holidays, Thanksgiving and Christmas. I discovered a long time ago that no matter how harsh Winter may be, we must persevere and endure it to make it to Springtime. We cannot hibernate or stop functioning because of what the Winter season brings.

The cycle of seasons is a recurring pattern that happens every year. As time advances, we see the characteristics of these seasons changing from their original nature and climate that we have been accustomed to. The changes, in part, have been blamed on global warming. However, we know that God is in control, and nothing happens unless He allows it to.

Just as the seasons change climate wise, our personal seasons change in life. Which season are you currently in? Is it Springtime in your life, wherein you are coming out of your shell and blossoming forth? Is it Summertime, wherein you have blossomed in full bloom and are spiraling in abundance and overcoming victory? Is it Fall time, wherein you were prospering but have now found yourself losing out on things you thought you had full possession of and control over? Or is it Winter in your life, wherein you feel all alone, deprived, and lack the hope you once had?

Child of God, just as each season comes and goes, your winter season will not last. Therefore, you do not have to wallow in self-pity or be as men most miserable without hope. When you are feeling distraught and powerless, this is the time you rely wholly on God's sustaining power and promises. I used to hear my late bishop, Bishop Cody V. Marshall say, "When you're at home feeling down or low in spirit, just lift your hands to the Lord and say, "Yes, Lord, yes, Lord." He promised that if we do this, the Lord will come in and lift our spirit, and before we realize it, we will be singing and praising God. *"For the joy of the Lord is your strength."* (Nehemiah 8:10b)

David indited in Psalm 121:1, *"I will lift up mine eyes to the hills, from whence cometh my help. My help cometh from the Lord, which made heaven and earth."* In verses 3 through 8, the version changes from the need of help to the promise of God's protection. So, when we are feeling down and in distress, who should we look to for help? Jesus! He is the lifter of our head and will comfort us and roll our burden away.

I remember several years ago it was just a few days after I had my right knee replacement surgery. My husband was at work, and I was home alone sitting in the dark when the spirit of loneliness and abandonment came over me. At that point, I felt like no one cared about me or the pain I was suffering. While sobbing uncontrollably, I began to call on the name of Jesus. I called on that great name because He promised to answer when we call unto Him. (Read Jeremiah 33:3)

When my husband arrived home a short time later, I was still sitting in the dark weeping and calling on the name of Jesus. He asked me what was wrong. I told him that I was praying and calling on Jesus for my help and consolation. He tried to console me, but at that moment only Jesus could comfort me like none other. This literally took place during a winter month, but it also felt like I was in my own personal winter season as well. Thank God, Winter does not last always.

Jesus lifted my burden and replaced my despair with joy, peace, and gratification. Child of God, we must not allow the enemy to deposit negative words into our spirit. He speaks nothing good, only words of defeat, despair, discouragement, and doubt. His primary goal is to steal our peace, kill our joy, and destroy the plan God has for our life. But thanks be to God, my pity party turned into a time of rejoicing because I realized how blessed I truly was. I had a loving and caring family, and of course, the surgery was a success, and I was on the road to a complete recovery.

In Psalm 46:1, the Word reassures us that, *"God is our refuge and strength, a very present help in trouble."* In this life trouble is liable to pop up its debilitating head at any time during any season. Therefore, it does not matter which season we are in, we still may have to face trouble. It is during these times we must be vigilant and trust God to be our present help and wait on His delivering power to bring us out victoriously. Remember, *"We are more than conquerors through him that loved us."* Apostle Paul also declared in Romans 8:28, *"For we know that all things work together for good to them that love God, to them who are the called according to his purpose."*

Whatever we may be going through certainly might not look or feel good, but it is working together for our good. God is preparing us for better, and when we get a little weak along the way, ask Him to increase our faith and for strength to endure the battle as a good soldier. It is not always easy to deal with life struggles, but with God on our side, we can overcome them.

I have shared at length details about the four natural seasons relating to their nature, various climates, and seasonal events. Furthermore, I have also alluded to events we cope with while in the various seasons of life. Perhaps if we could, I believe we would jump from one season to another for the sake of convenience, but that is not possible. God has set the seasons in place, both geologically and divinely. Therefore, we, the believers, await with great anticipation for the fifth season: our due season, our comeback season, our season of abundance, our season of overflow, our net breaking season, our season of miracles, or our season of supernatural favor.

Before we enter our fifth season, we must endure the pre-season, a season of tests and trials. *"Wherein ye greatly rejoice, though now for a season, if need be, ye are in heaviness (distressed) through manifold temptations."* (1 Peter 1:6)

2

The Pre-Season

And let us not be weary in well doing: for in Due
Season we shall reap, if we faint not.

(Galatians 6:9)

Every child of God has a fifth season if they do not give up, give in, or give out. This is one of God's promises to us in His Word. He created this season for His faithful followers. However, during the pre-season we must endure disappointments, hurts, and grief amid other struggles that might transpire before we enter our fifth season. Surely, I believe the fifth season (our due season) is the appointed time for the Child of God to reap a harvest of blessings. It is the time for us to be the head and not the tail, above and not beneath. It is the time for us to be the lenders and not borrowers. It is the time to experience the supernatural favor of God in our lives.

In Galatians 6:9, Apostle Paul was not speaking solely to us, but included himself as well. This lets us know that Paul was not merely encouraging the reader, but he reminded himself that we all have a due season to look forward to if we do not faint or give up. I believe Apostle Paul is encouraging us to hold on to our faith in God.

Our fifth season may be delayed but it is not denied. Therefore, I encourage you to hold on to God's unchanging hand and stay in the ship while riding through the storm. If we trust God during our tests and trials, including the dreadful global pandemic the world has been experiencing; and praise Him while we are going through, we are going to reap a bountiful harvest in the fifth season.

Apostle Paul also declared in 2 Corinthians 4:8, *"We may be troubled on every side, yet not distressed; perplexed, but not in despair; persecuted, but not forsaken; cast down, but not destroyed."* In this life, we are going to encounter trouble, but amidst the trouble, God promised that He would be with us. His goodness and mercy shall follow us all the days of our lives. For those who have experienced or are yet dealing with grief and sorrow because of the loss of loved ones, especially during the pandemic that has stricken so many, I pray that God's healing power will continue to sustain, comfort, and strengthen you. I reckon that each of us has been affected by the coronavirus, sorrow, or challenges in one way or another. But thanks be to God, trouble does not last always.

Let us remain steadfast and unmovable, clinging to our victory in the Lord. Solomon shared in Proverbs 24:10, *"If thou faint in the day of adversity, thy strength is small."* If you feel yourself getting weak, reach out to a prayer partner and ask them to pray with and for you.

"The effectual fervent prayer of a righteous man availeth much." (James 5:16b) When you, the child of God, pray, He will answer and give you strength and tenacity to outlast the storm. Remember, this too shall pass.

> **"Hast thou not known? Hast thou not heard that the everlasting God, the Lord, the Creator of the ends of the earth, fainteth not, neither is weary? There is no searching of his understanding. He giveth power to the faint; and to them that have no might he increaseth strength. Even the youths shall faint and be weary, and the young men shall utterly fall: But they that wait upon the Lord shall renew their strength; they shall mount up with wings as eagles; they shall run, and not be weary; and they shall walk, and not faint."** (Isaiah 40:28-31)

In Matthew 7:7, Jesus said, *"Ask, and it shall be given you; seek, and ye shall find; knock, and it shall be opened unto you. Everyone that asketh receiveth; and he that seeketh findeth, and to him that knocketh it shall be opened."* Please allow me to remind you again that this is not the time to faint, but while seeking the Lord for your deliverance, it is the perfect time to declare victory over the enemy of despair, discouragement, doubt, and unbelief. *"I had fainted, unless I had believed to see the goodness of the Lord in the land of the living."* (Psalm 27:13) How many times have we seen the Lord's goodness demonstrated in our lives? We have certainly witnessed His goodness over and over again. God is good all the time, and all the time God is good. Just ask Him, and you shall receive.

You are on God's calendar, and I honestly believe that most of you who are reading this book are on the brink of your fifth season, but the devil wants to discourage you and cause you to give up before reaching it. He has spoken lies into your ears and tried to set up roadblocks to keep you from entering your season of more than enough, which is rightfully yours. He has blind-sided you and are attacking your mental state of mind. In the pre-season you may well suffer being lied on, criticized, ostracized, or even rejected, but remember greater is He that is in you than he that is in the world. *"What shall we then say to these things? If God be for us, who can be against us?"* (Romans 8:31)

In Ephesians 6:11-12 Apostle Paul admonishes us to, *"Put on the whole armor of God, that ye may be able to stand against the wiles of the devil. For we wrestle not against flesh and blood, but against principalities, against powers, against the rulers of the darkness of this world, against spiritual wickedness in high places."* My brothers and sisters, we are engaged in a spiritual warfare; but understand that the battle is not ours, it's the Lord's. Let Jesus fight for you. When He fights our battle, it is an automatic win, win situation.

Let me also remind you of what Prophet Isaiah declared in Isaiah 54:17, *"No weapon that is formed against thee shall prosper; and every tongue that rise against thee in judgment, thou shalt condemn. This is the heritage of the servants of the Lord, and their righteousness is of me, saith the Lord."* Weapons will be formed against you, but they will not prosper. You are already a winner. You are the victor and not the victim. You are an overcomer. *"But thanks be to God, which giveth us the victory through our Lord Jesus Christ."* (1 Corinthians 15:57)

Jesus profoundly states in the Word of God that the devil is not just a liar, but he is the father of lies. (Read John 8:44) So, are you going to believe a lie, or are you going to believe the truth? In John 10:10, Jesus said, *"The thief cometh not, but for to steal, and to kill, and to destroy: I am come that they might have life, and that they might have it more abundantly."* Jesus came that we may have everlasting life as well as enjoy the abundance of life right here on earth.

It is the will of God that we flourish physically, spiritually, mentally, emotionally, and financially. However, we must follow the blueprint Joshua outlines in Joshua 1:8. *"This book of the law shall not depart out of thy mouth; but thou shalt meditate therein day and night, that thou mayest observe to do according to all that is written therein: for then thou shalt make thy way prosperous, and then thou shalt have good success."* Read God's Word. Meditate on God's Word. Obey God's Word. Speak God's Word. Then you shall prosper and be successful in a good way.

My brothers and sisters, when it does not look or feel like you are on the brink of your breakthrough, this is the time for your faith to kick in, and for you to take a stand on the Word of God and declare victory over the enemy in the mighty matchless name of Jesus. I heard a pastor say, "Change your words, change your life." In essence, your blessings are in your mouth. By faith speak it and God will bring it to pass.

Say to yourself, **"I am on the threshold of my due season. Despite sickness, sorrow, hurt and disappointment, I will hold on to God's unchanging hand. I am on the brink of a break-through to my Fifth Season.**

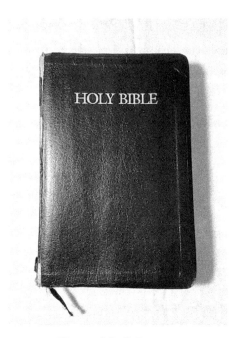

Home of God's Promises

By faith, I see you on God's calendar and your appointment is nearer than you can imagine. As Bishop Charles E. Blake, Sr., the Presiding Bishop Emeritus, C.O.G.I.C., often quotes, "I see you in the future and you look much better than you do right now." Glory to God!

*"I see you in the future and you look much
better than you do right now."*

Bishop Charles E. Blake, Sr.

Presiding Bishop Emeritus,

Church Of God In Christ, Inc.

3

You're Going to Live to See It Happen

Weeping may endure for a night,
but joy cometh in the morning.

(Psalm 30:5b)

God takes us through to get us to our Due Season. Does this statement make sense to you? I remember some years ago when my husband and I were going through a very lean financial period in our lives. When I say it was a rough time, that is putting it mildly. I remember how we would get down on our knees and cry out to the Lord and ask Him to come and rescue us. When I became discouraged during that season, my husband would encourage me. When he became despondent, I was there to uplift his spirit. Through all of this our love grew stronger and our deep appreciation for each other's devotion was amazing.

The songwriter wrote, "Our tests and trials only come to make us strong." Well, that is, if we do not faint, but overcome them triumphantly. Only then will they build our character and make us stronger.

Have you ever felt like you were in a hole so deep that it seemed like there was no help in getting out of it? Well, that was the place we found ourselves in at that time. It seemed like the world around us was caving in, and there was no help to be found. We even wondered if the Lord was with us amid this trial. Just as Job disclosed in Job 23:8-10, *"Behold, I go forward, but he is not there; and backward, but I cannot perceive him: On the left hand, where he doth work, but I cannot behold him; he hideth himself on the right hand, that I cannot see him. But he knoweth the way that I take: when he hath tried me, I shall come forth as gold."* Thank God, He was there all the time.

In James 1:2-4 he pens these words, *"My brethren, count it all joy when ye fall into divers temptations; Knowing this, that the trying of your faith worketh patience. But let patience have her perfect work, that ye may be perfect and entire, wanting nothing."* Our spirits were lifted, and we believed our change was going to happen. In our prayers to the Lord, we began to ask Him to help us to hold out until our change comes. We did not stop praying and fasting and believing God for our turn around season, our season of promise.

One day we decided we would just get away from it all and take an overnight trip. We did not have enough money to do what was needed to be done. So, we figured what would it hurt if we just took a few dollars and slip away. My husband, Thaddeus, suggested that we take an overnight trip to Wisconsin Dells. Well, that sounded okay to me until I heard the Lord say, "Go to Detroit, Michigan and attend the Greater Grace Temple Sunday service." I shared with my husband what the Lord had said and at first, he was somewhat hesitant about going. But then he agreed that it would be different and perhaps, more uplifting than a leisure trip.

We arrived in Detroit on Saturday afternoon, booked a room, dined out and relaxed during the remainder of the evening. On Sunday morning, we got up, showered, and got dressed and went to church not knowing what to expect. This was the first time we attended service in their beautiful new sanctuary, and when I say the spirit of the Lord moved mightily in that service, I am not exaggerating.

The mime group danced to the song, "Yes!" performed by the Shekinah Glory choir. Some of the words narrated by the soloist before the choir sang were:

"All God wants is a yes from us. If He told you what He really needed, will you still say yes? Will your heart and soul say yes? Will your spirit still say yes? There is more that I require of thee. Will your heart and soul say yes? My soul says yes. My mind says yes. My heart says yes. I will do what you want me to do. I'll say what you want me to say."

Wow! All God wants is a yes. I know some folks do not care much about this type of worship, but this group was so anointed; and when they finished, the church went up in a shout of praise and victory dance! We had a glorious time in the Lord. But hey wait, it was not over yet.

The pastor, Bishop Charles Ellis got up to preach, and I believe the title of his sermon was, "You Are On God's Calendar," (Read Habakkuk 2:1-4.) During his sermon, he used the illustration of a sick woman who called the doctor because she was in so much pain and felt like she was dying. She explained to the doctor about the excruciating pains she was experiencing and insisted that she needed to come see him.

However, the doctor told her to take a couple of pills and make an appointment to come see him in the future. Even though she insisted on seeing him right away, he remained unwavering and told her that he believed she could hold out until her appointment. Sometimes we might not feel that we can hold out until God turns things around for us. But God knows how much we can bear, and with His help we can hold out!

I may be paraphrasing it somewhat, but I heard Bishop Ellis say, "Some of you are going through tough times right now. Some of your bodies might even be in pain as I speak. Some might be having financial struggles, but no matter what you are going through, I want to encourage you to hold on to your faith in God, because God has you on His Calendar. And when the date of your appointment arrives, God is going to turn things around for you. He is going to give you beauty for your ashes, the oil of joy for your mourning, and the garment of praise for your heaviness. (Read Isaiah 61:3) It will be your season of overflow." Wow! We looked at each other in amazement and knew that God brought us there to hear that Rhema Word sent from heaven. On that Sunday we sowed a special seed offering, believing God for a financial revolution.

It was only a few weeks later that God opened the windows of heaven and poured us out a blessing we did not have room enough to receive it. Malachi 3:11 reads, *"And I will rebuke the devourer for your sakes, and he shall not destroy the fruits of your ground; neither shall your vine cast her fruit before the time in the field, saith the Lord of hosts. And all nations shall call you blessed: for ye shall be a delightsome land, saith the Lord of hosts."* God gave us strength to hold out until our appointment. Just think about it. What if we had thrown in the towel and given up on God? We would have missed our fifth season of restoration and abundance. It was indeed a net breaking season for us, and the people called us blessed. And indeed, we were a blessing to many.

What if Joseph had thrown in the towel during the twelve years, he spent in prison for something he did not do? He would have missed his fifth season.

On top of the Cloud Gate "The Bean" in Chicago

Because he did not give in to the enemy's conspiracies, God ultimately placed him at the head, a place of plenty where he would become a blessing to his father and the brothers that betrayed him and set him up to fail. Joseph's dilemma was a set up for God to show up and show out. *"And we know that all things work together for good to them that love God, to them who are the called according to his purpose."* (Romans 8:28) In the end God will place you in position for your enemies to see you on top. When the people see the end results, they will know that God did it.

Child of God, I would like to interject this admonition. If God has blessed you with a job or other means of income, pay your tithe to your local church. In giving the tithe you, the believer, put yourself in the position of obedience and subjection to God's plan for your life. (Read Malachi 3:8-11.) Tithing to your local church is the practice of giving 10 percent of one's income to the Lord. And in God's own timing, He will open the windows of heaven on your behalf and pour you out a blessing that you do not have enough room to receive it. My husband, Pastor Thaddeus Pitts, repeats these words every Sunday before receiving the tithe and offering, "Your offering is your seed. And when you plant your seed into good ground, expect to receive a great harvest."

I do not know who you are that is on the brink of giving up, but the Word of God tells us to not be weary in well doing, for in due season we are going to reap a harvest if we do not faint. *"Cast not away therefore your confidence, which hath great recompense of reward. For ye have need of patience, that, after ye have done the will of God, ye might receive the promise."* (Hebrews 10:35-36) If God has your appointed time of harvest on His calendar, you will not die before you see it happen.

Have you heard the song, "Live, Live, Live, Live, Live," performed by J. J. Hairston? It truly ministers, decrees, and declares life to your mind, soul, and body. Listen carefully to the prolific words of the song and allow it to minister to your spirit; and I promise that you will be inspired to live and not die. You will be motivated to trust God the more, and wait for His Promises to be fulfilled.

If the Lord has made you a promise, you're going live to see it happen. You can never be too old to have a fifth season. It is the season that is due you. You've been faithful and it is one of God's promises to you if you do not quit. Live, tell of His goodness, and reap all the benefits you have coming to you. Say emphatically as the Psalmist declares, *"I shall not die, but live, and declare the works of the Lord."* (Psalm 118:17) Believe it, expect it, and wait on it.

Yes, look forward to entering into your new season of overflow, and it will come to pass. God is working a miracle just for you, and when your date arrives, you will walk through the door of restoration and abundance. And it's going to be BIG! Better is coming! Greater is coming! Glory!

4

Stay On Faith Street

Faith is the substance of things hoped for;
the evidence of things not seen.

But without faith it is impossible to please Him.

For he that cometh to God must believe that He is; and
that He is a rewarder of them that diligently seek Him.

(Hebrews 11:1, 6)

If our God can turn night into day, He can turn your burdens into blessings. If our God can change water into wine, He can turn your negative situation into a positive outcome. If God can slow the rotation of the earth, so Joshua would have more time to defeat his enemies (Joshua 10:12-14), He has the perfect timing of your breakthrough. If our God can speak to the winds and the waves and say peace be still; and they obey; He can command blessings to overtake you, and they will obey. *"Though thy beginning was small, yet thy latter end should greatly increase."* (Job 8:7)

In Job 42:10, 12-13, we read where in the latter end of Job, after enduring such unimaginable suffering and devastating losses, after being criticized and ostracized by his so-called friends, God gave him double for his trouble. *"And the Lord turned the captivity of Job, when he prayed for his friends: also the Lord gave Job twice as much as he had before."* He was blessed with twice as much as he had in the beginning. Job received double for his trouble. The 17th verse tells us that Job lived a long full life to enjoy the blessings of God, *"So Job died, being old and full of days."* Read Job 1:2-3 verses to see what he had in the beginning and what God blessed him with at the end.

As Bishop T. D. Jakes would say, "Get ready, get ready, get ready to receive what God has for you. What God has for you it is for you. Jeremiah 29:11 reads, *"For I know the thoughts that I think toward you, saith the Lord, thoughts of peace, and not of evil, to give you an expected end."* God wants to give you hope and a future. Be assured that what's to come is better than what's been. He promised to restore what the enemy has taken. No one, not even the devil in hell can alter God's plans for your life.

Well, I had almost completed the manuscript for this book, when I heard my bishop, Bishop E. M. Walker, deliver a powerful and encouraging message for the International Men Perfecting Men Conference entitled, "Watch My Comeback," (Jeremiah 30:17-19). It was simply a confirmation of everything God had inspired me to share within this book. Bishop Walker declared that God was going to give us a comeback in our health, peace, finances, praise, dance, and more. We are going to be better, bigger, and stronger, and God will get the glory. Bishop Walker proceeded saying, "You saw my setback, now watch my comeback." Not once but twice God gave me confirmation through him and others that He had ordained the inspiring words written in this book. Come on and get excited, because your setback is only a setup for God to give you a comeback.

"You saw my setback.

Now watch my comeback."

Bishop E. M. Walker, NIJ, C.O.G.I.C. Prelate

I see increase and greater for you. What do you see for your-self? We must trust God while going through the pre-season process. In Ephesians 3:20, Paul declares, *"Now unto Him that is able to do exceeding, abundantly above all that we ask or think according to the power that worketh in us."* We serve a God who can do the impossible and unthinkable. Just one Word from Him can cause your mind-blowing miracle to come forth. Just one Word! He can res-urrect your dead situation just like Jesus did when He caused life to come back into dead Lazarus' body. What God can do has not even enter your mind. You have not even thought about asking for what He has in store for you. Draw from the faith power that is within you. Believe it, receive it, and wait on it, because your fifth season is only one appointment away.

"What didn't turn in your favor will
work for your good. Trust God."

Pastor Naamon Williams, Bread of Life C.O.G.I.C.

Perhaps you have heard Steve Harvey tell the story that Pastor Joel Osteen shared with him. The story is about a man who went to Heaven and was walking down the aisle way with Peter to a corridor. And when they got to the corridor, there were a lot of doors that had names on them. The man noticed the doors with the names on them and asked Peter what was behind those doors. Peter told him not to concern himself about those doors. And so, they continued to walk on.

Then they came to this one door that had the man's name on it. And the man said, "Whoa, Peter, this door has my name on it. Is there something I need to know about this door?" And Peter told the man, "No, don't worry about it. You are here now. So, just go on in and talk with Him." And the man said, "No, I want to see what's behind this door with my name on it." So Peter told him to go ahead and open the door. The man opened the door and in it was a large warehouse full of shelves, and on the shelves were packages with this man's name on them. And the man asked Peter, "What are all these boxes with my name on them?" And Peter told the man that these are all the blessings and all the things God wanted to ship to you when you were on earth, but...

1. Each time God had a blessing for you, you did not ask Him for it. And in His Word, He told you to ask, and it shall be given, but you did not ask. And so, you received not because you asked not.

2. Each time God had a blessing for you, you did not believe that you could have it. Instead, you doubted it. And so,

because of doubt, you received not because you asked not. And,

3. Each time God had a blessing for you, you did not feel that you were worthy of His blessings. And so, because you did not feel you were worthy of His blessings, you received not because you asked not.

And Peter told him, "So all these packages and blessings you could have had are yet up here in God's warehouse." After the man saw what he had missed out on while on earth, he wished he had never gone into that room.

Steve proceeded to say, "To receive what God has for you, you must be in the right place at the right time with the right frame of mind. Do not be afraid to ask for it. You cannot move from Faith Street to Doubt It Drive. You cannot move off Faith Street to Pity Party Way. You cannot move off Faith Street to It's Not Meant to Be for Me Lane. You cannot move off Faith Street to I Ain't Worthy Boulevard."

> *But let him ask in faith, nothing wavering. For he that wavereth is like a wave of the sea driven with the wind and tossed. For let not that man think that he shall receive any thing of the Lord. A double-minded man is unstable in all his ways.*
> (James 1:6-8)

Don't get sidetracked. You must remain on FAITH Street to receive what God has for you. If you give up on God and waiver in your faith, your box will be sent back to the Sender, and you will have a warehouse full of packages and blessings up there with your name on it that you never received. *"Let them shout for joy, and be glad, that favour my righteous cause: yea, let them say continually, Let the Lord be magnified, which hath pleasure in the prosperity of his servant."* (Psalm 35:27)

I do not know about you, but by faith I am claiming everything that God's got for me and more. If it is peace, I want it. If it is joy, I want it. If it is deliverance, I want it. If it is healing, I want it. If it is a new house, I want it. If it is a new car, I want it. Whatever it is, I name it and claim it and receive it in Jesus' name. Lord, help me to stay on Faith Street. For we walk by faith and not by sight. Remember the three F's: faith, favor, and finances.

In James 1:6, he said when you ask of God, ask Him in faith, with nothing wavering. And James goes on to say, *"Let not that man think that he shall receive any thing of the Lord."* Hebrews 10:35-36 instructs us to, *"Cast not away therefore your confidence, which have great recompense of reward. For ye have need of patience, that, after ye have done the will of God, ye might receive the promise."* After you have asked, be patient while waiting on the manifestation thereof. *"My soul, wait thou only upon God; for my expectation (hope) is from him. He only is my rock and my salvation; he is my defense; I shall not be greatly moved."* (Psalm 62:5-6)

He may not come when you want Him to, but He is never late. God is always on time. And it is your faith that moves Him into action on your behalf. It is your faith that pleases God. Hebrews 11:6 declares, *"But without faith it is impossible to please Him; For he that cometh to God must believe that He is, and that He is a rewarder of them that diligently seek Him."* So again, wait patiently on Him while you seek Him.

In Matthew 21:21-22, *"Jesus answered and said unto them, Verily I say unto you, If ye have faith, and doubt not, ye shall not only do this which is done to the fig tree, but also if ye shall say unto this mountain, Be thou removed, and be thou cast into the sea, it shall be done. And all things, whatsoever ye shall ask in prayer, believing, ye shall receive."* In John 14:13, Jesus promised, *"And whatsoever ye shall ask in my name, that will I do, that the Father may be glorified in the Son."* What are you waiting for? Ask for what you want from the Lord. The invitation has been given; and the promise has been made. Think about it. Are you holding up your own blessings by not asking? Are you holding up your own blessings by having unforgiveness in your heart? *"Therefore I say unto you, What things soever ye desire when ye pray, believe that ye receive them, and ye shall have them. And when ye stand praying, forgive, if ye have aught against any: that your Father also which is in heaven may forgive you your trespasses."* (Mark 11:24-25)

God has given me blessings that I could have never imagined I would enjoy. God has opened doors for me that I never thought would be opened. He has healed my body when the specialist and surgeon were so sure that I had cancer. God had already spoken and said that there would be no cancer in my body. Therefore, I did not believe the doctor nor surgeon's reports. By faith I believed the report of the Lord. I had nodules located on both sides of my thyroid gland. The largest and most suspicious looking one was located awfully close to my vocal cord. Because of this, the surgeon forewarned me on the very day of my thyroidectomy that he could not guarantee that I would be able to speak after the surgery. But God!

When I went back for my post-surgery appointment, the Specialist smiled and said to me, "Lottie, you are our first." I asked him what he meant about me being their first. He said, "You are our first patient that we were very suspicious of having cancer, based on what we saw on the x-rays, that came back from surgery cancer free." Glory to God! I later found out from the surgeon that he had actually performed two surgeries on me that day. Not only did he remove my thyroid gland, but he also removed two lymph nodes from my neck to check for cancer. NO cancer.

Let me tell you that not only was I talking after surgery, but I came out of recovery giving God the praise. There is no secret what God can do. What He has done for me and others, He can do for you. I have no clue what you may be facing, the hurt you may feel, or the struggles you are going through, but I pray that this scripture will give you courage and strength to make it through the process. *"Fear thou not; for I am with thee: be not dismayed; for I am thy God: I will strengthen thee; yea, I will help thee; yea, I will uphold thee with the right hand of my righteousness."* (Isaiah 41:10) The Lord is with you and will give you strength to overcome. He will turn it around in your favor.

"In everything give thanks: for this is the will of God in Christ Jesus concerning you." (1 Thessalonians 5:18) It is the will of God that we give Him what He certainly deserves, and that is to give Him

praise and tell Him, "Thank you." I praise Him every chance I get, and I encourage you not to wait until your fifth season arrives, but to give God praise now. Praise Him for your miracle. Praise Him for your healing. Praise Him for your breakthrough. Praise Him for your loved one's salvation and deliverance. Praise Him before the manifestation takes place. *"Praise him for his mighty acts: praise him according to his excellent greatness."* (Psalm 150:2)

When I think about the goodness of Jesus and all that He has done for me, my soul cries out Hallelujah, thank God for saving me. My brothers and sisters, we got a right to praise God. When I think about all that He has done for me and my family and our church family, and when I open my mouth to praise Him, I realize that I owe God that and so much more. When your praises go up, God and His blessings will show up.

A Grateful Soul

5

Season of Recovery and Restoration

And David recovered all that the Amalekites had carried away: and David rescued his two wives. And there was nothing lacking to them, neither small nor great, neither sons nor daughters, neither spoil, nor any thing that they had taken to them: David recovered all.

(1 Samuels 30:18-19)

At the beginning of 2021 God gave me a message entitled, "2021, The Year of Your Recovery." Well, I believe God is yet bringing this affirmation to past, even in 2022. Therefore, I hope and pray that in this year and henceforth, whatever the enemy has taken from you, you will recover that and more. Just keep the faith and persevere. The power of prayer, praise, and perseverance shall prevail. Your praise, faith, and action move God.

My grandfather, the late Dr. Theodore R. Jackson, always taught on Faith from the Eleventh chapter of Hebrews. One day someone asked him why he taught on faith so much. His reply was, "I am going to keep teaching on Faith until everyone's faith increases. Until then I am not going to stop." *"So then faith cometh by hearing, and hearing by the word of God."* (Hebrews 10:17)

In James 2:14, 17-18, 26 he penned, *"What doth it profit, my brethren, though a man say he hath faith, and have not works? Can faith save him? Even so faith, if it hath not works, is dead, being alone. Yea, a man may say, Thou hast faith, and I have works: show me thy faith without thy works, and I will show thee my faith by my works. For as the body without the spirit is dead, so faith without works is dead also."* In this passage of scripture James' message is clear and simple. Put some action with your faith and watch God change things.

In Joel 2:25-26, God promises us that He will give us a season of restoration and restore not weeks or months, but years that the enemy has deprived us of. And He will replace them with a season of more than enough. Your joy will be restored. Careers will be restored. Marriages will be restored. Families will be restored, and relationships will be restored.

> *"And I will restore to you the years that the locust hath eaten, the cankerworm, and the caterpillar, and the palmerworm, my great army which I sent among you. And ye shall eat in plenty, and be satisfied, and praise the name of the Lord your God, that hath dealt wondrously with you: and my people shall never be ashamed."* (Joel 2:25-26)

I Samuel 30:6 tells us how David and his men grieved after the Amalekites came while they were away and stole all their possessions, took their wives and all their sons and daughters; and burned the city. As if that was not bad enough, David was put under a lot of extra pressure and stress because he heard that his own men wanted to kill him. It certainly was a winter season in David's life.

But the good part about it, even amid this troublesome time, the Bible tells us that David encouraged himself in the Lord. Well, am I addressing any self-encouragers? **When you encourage yourself, it enables you to become energized, revitalized, rejuvenated, and motivated.** And I don't know about you, but I discovered that sometimes when things are in the worst way, and there is no one else around to encourage you; this is the time when you have to muster up enough strength to encourage yourself in the Lord.

Have you ever experienced hurt, disappointment, and abandonment? Has your heart been broken? Are you grieving or in distressed? Well my brother and sister, do not try to carry these burdens alone. Allow me to encourage you to cast your cares upon Jesus. For He genuinely cares for you; and your recovery is in progress. "*Casting all your care upon him; for he careth for you.*" (1 Peter 5:7) Jesus loves you and cares for you.

Prayer Still Works

Heads up, you are too blessed to be stressed, and you do not want to be a participant in the devil's pity party. The only thing we want to do is to command the enemy to get thee hence in the mighty matchless name of Jesus. So child of God, rise, dust yourself off, and seek the Lord for your turn-around miracle. Jesus said, *"Call unto me, and I will answer thee, and show thee great and mighty things, which thou knowest not."* (Jeremiah 33:3)

This is exactly what David did. Yes, it was a stressful time for him. Even in the midst of the grief and heartache, David sought the Lord on whether he should pursue after the troops. The Lord told David yes, pursue, and he would overtake the enemy, and recover all that they had stolen from him. Praise God! And the Bible tells us that David pursued as the Lord had instructed him to, and he did what? He recovered all. When I say he recovered all, I mean everything, including their wives, sons, and daughters, and all their possessions, great or small, and the spoil. Restoration had finally come. David did not allow fear or stress to get in the way of his recovery.

"For God hath not given us the spirit of fear, but of power, and of love, and of a sound mind." (2 Timothy 1:7) Do not allow the spirit of fear take control when you are in the midst of a crisis. Fear could become an obstacle to your blessings and success if you allow it to. I heard someone say that your destiny is guarded by fear. So if you have to, break through that barrier of fear, and pursue what's rightfully yours. By faith, you shall recover all. Remember, it takes courage to handle adversity.

At the very beginning of 2020 God said that it would be a year of increase, which I shared with the People of God at my church. My brothers and sisters, God is a promise keeper, and if He said it, you could bank on it. In 2020 we witnessed the saving of souls, God opening doors, new job opportunities, promotions, salary increases, provision of food in abundance, and so much more amid the Covid-19 pandemic. And the good part about it, I don't believe He is through blessing His people yet. There is more to come.

His favor and blessings spilled over into 2021. David notated in Psalm 37:25-26, *"I have been young, and now I am old; yet have I not seen the righteous forsaken, nor his seed begging bread. He is ever merciful, and lendeth; and his seed is blessed."* With our own eyes, we have seen God's children fed, clothed, and flourished even in the midst of a season of woes (grief or troubles).

Child of God, you are included in the lineup for God's promised season of blessings. This could be the season of not only experiencing an abundance of finance, but an abundance of life, joy, peace, and supernatural favor. I believe that this year could be the year for God's children to reap a harvest of blessings and take back what the enemy has stolen from us. I don't just mean what he took in 2020, but in time past as well. God always fulfills His promises.

I also believe this is the year of Ministry that God is calling for. I believe God is commissioning us to witness to lost souls like never before, that they may repent and be saved before it is too late. *"The fruit of the righteous is a tree of life; and he that winneth souls is wise. Behold, the righteous shall be recompensed (rewarded) in the earth much more than the wicked and the sinner."* (Proverbs 11:30-31) Yes, I believe this is the season of Spiritual and Financial manifestations; the season of Repossession and Reclamation!

Not only did the Lord keep His promise to David but He revealed Himself to me once again as the Promise Keeper. It began in 2019 when I was looking for a part time job. While I was looking for it, a full-time job opportunity was presented to me by Deshaun Wallace, a very dear friend and church member. I was really hesitant in applying for the position because I had been retired from a teaching career for several years. Therefore, I was not even sure if I would be capable of working full time again, as well as getting up so early every morning to go to work. But how many of you know when the Lord is in the plan, you got to move? Nevertheless, yes Lord.

Despite my apprehension I applied for the position. I submitted my resume and references and waited for a response. They liked what they saw, and I was called in for an interview. The interview went well, and now I was waiting for my background check to come back. For the time being I was praying and asking God if this was really Him. I soon discovered that it was indeed another set-up from God. God let me know that it was Him, and He promised that I would be able to pay my bills, do things that I dreamed of doing, and have money left over after I left the job.

To say the least, I got the job, and my salary was the most I ever made while working for someone else. I had not worked on a full-time job since 2005. All of this continued to evolve while in the pandemic. Believe me, it happened just the way He promised. Praise God! I am now happily retired again, which goes to show you that it does not take God a long, drawn-out period to give you your heart's desire. It was indeed another mind-blowing experience. Surely, we must trust God and take great pleasure in pleasing Him. *"Delight thyself also in the Lord; and he shall give thee the desires of your heart. Commit thy way unto the Lord; trust also in him; and he shall bring it to pass."* (Psalm 37:4-5)

God does what He wants to, how He wants to, and when He wants to. Just be in position to receive all that God has promised you in His Word. Name it and claim it. It is yours for the asking. It is yours, it's your blessing. It is your season to recover all. Enjoy! Truly, our God is a promise keeper.

6

Welcome to the Fifth Season

Season of Overflow –
Your Net Breaking Season

"And when they had this done, they enclosed a great multitude of fishes; and their net brake."

(Luke 5:6)

In the 5th Chapter of Luke, Jesus noticed two ships standing by the lake that had no fishermen on board, because they were washing their nets. In essence, they had finished fishing for the evening and were cleaning their nets without catching any fish. However, it was very timely for their ships to be docked and available for the master's use.

Because of Jesus' need for use of one of the ships to teach the people, He entered one of the boats that belonged to Simon. He asked him to thrust the ship out a little farther from the land, and Jesus sat down and began to teach the people from the ship. When he had finished teaching, He told Simon to, *"Launch out into the deep, and let down your nets for a draught (catch of fish)."*

"Your Net breaking Season."

When Jesus told Simon to launch out into the deep, Simon told him, *"Master, we have toiled all the night, and have taken nothing:* **nevertheless** *at thy word I will let down the net."* The Word of God affirms that, *"And when they had this done, they enclosed a great multitude of fishes; and their net brake."* Wow! What an amazing net breaking experience. Because of his obedience to the spoken word of Jesus, and his nevertheless attitude, in spite of how things looked, Simon Peter opened the door to his net breaking miracle. By faith speak your blessing into the atmosphere, and what looks impossible will become possible with God. Then watch God bring it to pass.

They beckoned unto their partners, which were in the other ship that they would come and help them with their draught. The other ship came and both ships were filled until their ships began to sink. When they saw what happened, they were astonished at all the fish they had taken in. Because of his obedience, the net breaking, mind blowing miracle happened; and Simon Peter welcomed his fifth season. After that great miracle, they became fishermen of men. They began to fish for souls, one of the most rewarding assignments a child of God could have. Your fifth season could be the precise time God has prepared you to not only reap the blessing of prosperity, but to fulfill a greater assignment from Him.

Nevertheless at Your word, because You said it, I believe it, and that settles it. Nevertheless at Your word, regardless of my past failures, I trust You, Lord and I will obey Your command. Nevertheless at Your word, no matter what I think, I am going to trust You and launch out into the deep. Nevertheless, I am going to journey into an unfamiliar territory because You are with me, and I will fear no evil. And Lord, when You open the windows of heaven and pour me out blessings that I do not have room enough to receive, the people will know that You did it. Decree and declare it today, and begin thanking God for your fifth season of overflow.

After we have tried everything, and everything has failed, try Jesus. He will make everything alright. Proverbs 3:5-6 reads, *"Trust in the Lord with all thine heart, and lean not unto thine own understanding. In all thy ways acknowledge him and he shall direct thy paths."*

If we trust the Lord (rely on Him), and lean not unto our own understanding, and acknowledge Him (have fellowship and relationship with God in all our ways), God will make straight the paths before us. Remember that obedience and endurance are the keys to our turn-around season.

While in your fifth season be a good steward over the financial blessings God has bestowed to you. Be a supporter of kingdom's ministries. Be a blessing to those who are less fortunate. Encourage someone else to take a leap of faith. Bring along a brother or sister while you enjoy the journey through your fifth season. Call and uplift someone's spirit while you are uplifted. Speak peace to their confused state of mind. Speak a word of inspiration to someone while they are trying to reach their goal. Be purpose driven in this season. Make someone else's day. Feed the hungry and give to the poor. Remember only what you do for Christ will last.

> *"Then shall the King say unto them on his right hand, Come, ye blessed of my Father, inherit the kingdom prepared for you from the foundation of the world: For I was an hungered (hungry) and ye gave me meat (food): I was thirsty, and ye gave me drink: I was a stranger, and ye took me in. Naked, and ye clothed me: I was sick, and ye visited me: I was in prison, and ye came unto me. Then shall the righteous answer him, saying, Lord, when saw we thee an hungered, and fed thee? Or thirsty, and gave thee drink? When saw we thee a stranger, and took thee in? or naked, and clothed thee? Or when*

saw we thee sick, or in prison, and came unto thee? And the King shall answer and say unto them, Verily I say unto you, In as much as ye have done it unto one of the least of these my brethren, ye have done it unto me. " (Matthew 25:34-40)

Just as the four natural seasons reoccur each year, fifth seasons reoccur as well. I have been blessed by God to experience a few fifth seasons in my life. God has favored me time and time again. The first major season of favor I recall is when the company I was working for back in the eighties was relocating to Dallas, Texas. I worked in the Human Resource Department and was asked to relocate with the company, but I turned down the offer. I had the option of remaining on until the company closed in September or exit early that May. I was led to leave early, and after my last day the young lady who was relocating with the company replaced me.

The following week I received a phone call from the secretary of the vice president in Human Resources informing me that the young lady did not work out. My boss was wondering if I would be willing to come back and work until the company relocated. I explained to her that I had started my own Temporary Agency, and if allowed, I would come back as an independent contractor under my agency's name. She spoke with my former boss, and he agreed to my terms and fee. This was a set up for God to show up, and it introduced my fifth season, and God gave me divine favor from that point on. In your fifth season, ask God for what you want, and you shall receive that and more. As the late Dr. Mattie Moss Clark would say, "I know I got that right."

One day while I was working on the computer, the supervisor from the Accounting Department came by and asked how my business was doing. I told her that it was doing okay. Mind you that I was my only temp at the time. She asked me if I could provide a temp for her department within the next two weeks while an employee goes on vacation. By faith I told her (by faith) no problem, I would have someone there by the requested date. On the following Sunday during our morning worship service, one of the young ladies in the choir testified how she was working as a temp in Schaumburg, Illinois. She was grateful for the job even though she had to commute a long distance to get there and was being paid a low hourly wage. It was during her testimony that the Holy Spirit spoke to me and said that she was my new temp.

After service that Sunday, I asked her how she would like to come work for me as a temp making more money per hour. She readily said yes and was happy to do so. Well, to make a long story short, during the next four months before the company relocated to Texas, God blessed me to hire seventeen temps besides myself to work around the clock. My tithe was as much as $400.00 a week (in the eighties) during that fifth season. "Praise God!" And yes, I paid my taxes. This testimony reminds me of the message I delivered in 2020, "Your Fifth Season Has Arrived." Truly, my fifth season had arrived and overtaken me. To God be the glory!

The first young lady I hired worked out so well, the company paid me to release her to relocate with them to Dallas. Besides her excellent office skills, God gave her favor with the supervisor. It was definitely a set-up from God. She was under the umbrella of God's favor raining down on me. The last I heard, she met one of the employees there in Dallas, fell in love and got married. This became her fifth season as well. It is wonderful to be connected to the right people. Won't He do it!

It did not stop there. As the time was approaching for the company to relocate, I was asked to go to Dallas to help the Human Resource Department set up their files, etc. They also wanted me to continue to commute back and forth between Dallas and Chicago each week. I prayerfully considered it but decided not to because I really could not leave my family every week for a week at a time, only to return home on weekends. Even though it was all expenses paid including my meals, hotel expenses, and a real nice bonus, I prayerfully declined. Besides that, I was not fond of being a frequent flyer living in a hotel.

My love and commitment to my family overshadowed their offer of a great salary and benefits. However, I did agree to go for one week and help the department set up their files. I was led by the Holy Spirit and influenced by my husband to not accept the offer, which I am so glad I obeyed. Less than a year later, most of the employees who relocated to Dallas, Texas had returned to Chicago. The company's merger failed.

"I have showed you all things, how that so laboring ye ought to support the weak, and to remember the words of the Lord Jesus, how he said, It is more blessed to give than to receive." (Acts 20:35) Yes, it is more blessed to have to give than to be on the receiving end. In your fifth season of abundance and overflow, you will be blessed to be a

blessing to others without any undisclosed agendas. For how can you bless others if you are not blessed?

"It is said that there is greater joy in giving than there is in receiving. But I have learned that it is only if the giving is without expectations, without hidden cost or without undisclosed agendas. If someone were to discuss your gift giving practices, what sort of spirit would they say you give from?"

Marcus C. Gentry

I shared my experience to not boast, but because I really want to encourage you who are waiting on God. Whether you're waiting on your healing, deliverance, a turnaround breakthrough, a job, a raise, a promotion, or whatever, God's timing is always the right time for your miracle. Only He can bring it to pass. So hold on, it will happen.

Since that first extraordinary fifth season, God has blessed me with others. Years later after raising our sons, I resumed my journey to pursue a bachelor's degree in Educational Administration at another university while working full time at Governors State University. Upon presenting my portfolio, I received extra credits for my past work experiences plus credit for the college points already earned. God blessed me to earn this degree in October 1997 after satisfactorily completing the required college correspondence courses.

In December 1997, Evangelical Christian School of Chicago hired me to fill the open position of a Fifth-grade schoolteacher, teaching all academic subjects and Bible. This was really a dream come true. Remember, it is never too late to pursue your dream. To God be the glory!

Before I continue to share the phase of another one of my fifth seasons, allow me to give you a little background information on how the favor of God was in my life. Another private Christian School in Chicago had offered me a Fourth-Grade teacher's position years before I completed college. However, I had to turn down the offer because I did not have a babysitter at the time. I was disappointed because I really wanted the job but later realized that it was not on God's calendar for my life. Not long after I was hired, the school closed. I thank God because it worked out for my good.

Truly, our God does things in a divine order. So, be patient and wait on Him. The only other teaching experience I had other than teaching Sunday School and Young People Willing Workers classes in the church for years was with Sawyer Business College in Chicago. At the college I taught typing and other office skills as a Teacher's Assistant. So, please do not take the jobs you hold in the ministry lightly. Those experiences and the supernatural favor of God could open doors to greater opportunities that seem impossible.

I began my full-time teaching career that following January after the Christmas Break. While teaching at ECS, God blessed me to earn an outstanding reputation as an excellent teacher, and my administrator recommended that I complete an application for the Golden Apple Teacher's Award. I was also selected to be the Chairperson over the Fourth and Fifth Grades Department. The Lord blessed me to teach for eight school years before I had to take an early retirement from teaching to provide care for my ailing grandmother. In the meantime, I continued tutoring in after school programs and started my own tutoring service, which was highly successful. My staff and I tutored in math and reading and provided homework assistance to students from Kindergarten through Sixth Grade. Again, won't He do it!

During that time, I designed and penned a manual for parents and grandparents as a tool to assist them in helping their children and grandchildren with their schoolwork and homework assignments. For years that manual was listed on the Church of God in Christ website under the Urban Initiatives heading as a resource material. Both my educational career and tutoring business lasted for a combined total of well over two decades. It was during this era that God blessed me to earn a master's degree in Christian Education and an Honorary Doctorate Degree as well.

Wow! if I tried to explain how God turned things around in my favor, you would not be able to comprehend the mystery of His supernatural favor in my life during that time. Not only did God bless me to see my dream of becoming a teacher since I was nine years old to become a reality, but He also blessed me to become a successful entrepreneur. **"But Jesus beheld them, and said unto them, With men this is impossible; but with God all things are possible."** (Matthew 19:26) Child of God, we serve a turn-around God who can do the impossible. So, never stop trusting Him to turn things around for you.

Please do not get the wrong idea. I have experienced many disappointments, hurt in the church, hurt in the family, sickness, and grief in between my fifth seasons. But thank God for the victories won. I also thank God because through it all He has never left me alone. He's had me on His Calendar each time, and in spite of what's to come, God promises to be with me. Remember, He promised to never leave us nor forsake us. Who would not serve a God like this?

7

Outpouring Of Oil Season

Now there cried a certain woman of the wives of the sons of the prophets unto Elisha, saying, Thy servant my husband is dead; and thou knowest that thy servant did fear the Lord: and the creditor is come to take unto him my two sons to be bondmen. And Elisha said unto her, What shall I do for thee? Tell me, what hast thou in the house? And she said, Thine handmaid hath not anything in the house, save a pot of oil.

Then he said, Go, borrow thee vessels abroad of all thy neighbors, even empty vessels; borrow not a few. And when thou art come in, thou shalt shut the door upon thee and upon thy sons, and shalt pour out into all those vessels, and thou shalt set aside that which is full. So she went from him and shut the door upon her and upon her sons, who brought the vessels to her; and she poured out.

And it came to pass, when the vessels were full, that she said unto her son, Bring me yet a vessel. And he said unto her, There is not a vessel more. And the oil stayed. Then she came and told the man of God. And he said, Go, sell the oil, and pay thy debt and live thou and thy children of the rest.

(2 Kings 4:1-7)

I have heard this message preached several times, but it was only when I read the entire scripture for myself, that it became an eye opener. This widow was in despair and in fear of losing her two sons to the creditor to work as slaves, in lieu of a debt her deceased husband owed. The poor woman was already grieving over the death of her husband; and now this. So, who could she turn to? She turned to Elisha, the man of God, for help. What a blessing it is to have a man or woman of God you can go to for direction and help in time of need. So love and appreciate them.

She explained her situation to him, and the prophet asked her, "What do you want me to do about it? What do you have in your house to help you get out of this misfortune?" Well, she could have responded by answering him with a question, "Excuse me, Elisha, what do you mean? I need your help, and not a lot of questions." Instead, she simply replied, "I have nothing but a pot of oil." Little did she know that that pot of oil was the prelude to her fifth season. It was a way out of her no way out. It was her ram in the bush.

Elisha told her to go and borrow as many empty vessels as possible that she could from all her neighbors. Notice that the man of God is telling her to go borrow from her neighbors, as if she was not already indebted to the creditor. Sometimes what the man or woman of God instructs us to do seems foolish, but if we would just obey them as they are led by Holy Spirit, we would see God work a miracle on our behalf. This was surely a set up for God to show up and show out on behalf of this widow.

Elisha proceeded to tell her that once she has gathered the vessels, he wanted her and her sons to shut the door and begin to pour oil out of that one pot (the miracle pot) into all the vessels that she had gathered. This miraculous provision was a spiritual experience and was not intended for the public to watch. For what God does in secret shall be revealed and rewarded openly, and then, only then, shall the people know that God did it.

The oil did not cease until all the vessels were completely full. She wanted to continue to pour out the oil, but her son told her, *"Mother, there are no more vessels."* Immediately, she went and reported the outpouring (the overflow) of oil miracle to the man of God. And he told her to go and sell the oil, and pay off her debt, and for her and her sons to live off the rest. Wow! How would you like to receive more than enough? So much so, until you have enough funds to pay off all your debt and be able to live off the rest? You don't have to work anymore nine to five jobs unless you want to. Truly, our God is a miracle worker. Do I have a witness? What an awesome provision this was from the Lord! *"But my God shall supply all your need according to his riches in glory by Christ Jesus."* (Philippians 4:19)

Children of God, you might not have much to work with, but use what you got. In your fifth season, God will take little and make much. He will give the increase. This is your turnaround season. For in Jesus Christ we have the victory. *"What shall we then say to these things? If God be for us, who can be against us? He that spared not his own Son, but delivered him up for us all, how shall he not with him also freely give us all things?"* (Romans 8:31-32) *"But thanks be to God, which giveth us the victory through our Lord Jesus Christ."* (1 Corinthians 15:57)

The Blessings of Obedience

And it shall come to pass, if thou shalt hearken diligently unto the voice of the Lord thy God, to observe and to do all his commandments which I command thee this day, that the Lord thy God will set thee on high above all nations of the earth: And all these blessings shall come on thee, and overtake thee, if thou shalt hearken unto the voice of the Lord thy God. Blessed shalt thou be in the city, and blessed shalt thou be in the field. Blessed shall be the fruit (offspring) of thy body, and the fruit of thy cattle, the increase of thy kine, and the flocks of thy sheep. Blessed shall be thy basket and thy store. Blessed shalt thou be when thou comest in, and blessed shalt thou be when thou goest out. The Lord shall cause thine enemies that rise up against thee

to be smitten (defeated) before thy face: they shall come out against thee one way and flee before thee seven ways. The Lord shall command the blessing upon thee in thy storehouses, and in all that thou settest thine hand unto; and he shall bless thee in the land which the Lord thy God giveth thee.
(Deuteronomy 28:1-8)

Well said and well received. Obedience to the Word of God and to the man or woman of God is the key to our fifth season of miracles and blessings. I remember being in their home tending to my grandmother, Dr. Naomi R. Jackson Goodwin, when Bishop Bennie E. Goodwin, Sr. asked me how my business was doing. I told him that it was doing okay. That morning he prophesied to me saying, "Daughter, the Lord is going to bless your business and whatsoever you set your hands to do." Do you not know that he spoke this prophecy before I experienced that awesome abundance of blessings in 1986; and since then the Lord has blessed me repeatedly. I shall never forget that profound prophecy spoken over my life by the man of God.

I also remember the prophecy given to me by Pastor Billy Jermale Evans in May 2015. He called me out before the people in a service and said that God was going to have someone bless me with a blessing that would blow my mind. Wow! Did my heart burn with in? He continued on to say that God said that not only one mind-blowing blessing will take place, but one after another one would occur. By that time, my heart was thrilled, and I rejoiced for my forthcoming blessings.

In 2016 God began to fulfill His promise. God blessed my husband to retire at the beginning of that year, and despite the obstacle we faced, God blessed him to pay cash for our new home out of his retirement funds. No, we do not live in an elaborate mansion, but it is a lovely (one of a kind) home in the community, which we love dearly and appreciate. It is located in a very quiet and well-groomed gated community. Sometimes when man says no, God says yes. Remember, He has the final say. While you are trying to figure it out, God has already worked it out. Since then one mind-blowing blessing after another has taken place. Hallelujah!

"Jabez cried out to the God of Israel saying, 'Oh that you would bless me and enlarge my territory! Let your hand be with me, and keep me from harm so that I will be free from pain.' And God granted his request." (1 Chronicles 4:10 NIV) In Jabez's prayer, he besought God to give him bigger and better things. In essence He was asking God to give him more authority and opportunity to bring glory to Him. This was his specific goal.

We have the same privilege to pray to our Father God and ask Him to bless us with bigger and better things. We also have the opportunity to ask Him to bless us with overflowing joy, peace that surpasses understanding, supernatural favor, and the empowerment to survive whatever lies ahead. Let us not be timid when praying. Come boldly before His throne of grace.

> *"Father God, enlarge my territory and expand my borders. Not only for myself but I ask that this favor be upon the lives of every believer that walks upright before you. I decree and declare that this*

is our season of greater. Cancel the contract of the enemy that comes to steal, kill, and destroy. Lord, save our loved ones. Cover our families with your blood, protect us, and keep us from all manner of sickness and diseases, hurt, harm, and danger in Jesus' name. Amen."

Congratulations on your Fifth Season! You did not faint but endured another pre-season as a good soldier. Therefore, God is now rewarding you for your labor of love and steadfastness. This is your season to be blessed. You have stood the test. Now stand still and see the manifestations of God's Promise to you. He's going to open up the windows of heaven and pour you out an abundance of blessings. This is your season to be blessed.

"Love My 5th Season" Bracelet

Child of God, if your Fifth Season has not arrived yet, hold on. It is closer than you think.

Power of the Tongue

Have you ever given thought to the words you say and the significant role they play in your life? Believe it not, our words can propel us to or deter our next fifth season. Because we want our words to have a positive impact on God and man, we must be conscience of our speech at all times. Our words can speak and release life or death, encouragement, or discouragement, good or evil, peace or confusion, healing or hurt into the atmosphere. Therefore, I am moved to share with you a few scriptures that may inspire you to choose your words wisely at all times, whether you are in a pre-season or fifth season.

> *"Death and life are in the power of the tongue: and they that love it shall eat the fruit thereof."* (Proverbs 18:21)

> *"Let the words of my mouth, and the meditation of my heart, be acceptable in thy sight, O Lord, my strength (my rock), and my redeemer."* (Psalm 19:14)

> *"Pleasant words are as a honeycomb, sweet to the soul, and health to the bones."* (Proverbs 16:24)

> *"A man hath joy by the answer of his mouth: and a word spoken (in its time) in due season, how good is it."* (Proverbs 15:23)

> *"Let no corrupt communication proceed out of your mouth, but that which is good to the use*

of edifying, that it may minister grace unto the hearers." (Ephesians 4:29)

"But I say unto you, That every idle word that men shall speak, they shall give account thereof in the day of judgment. For by thy words thou shalt be justified, and by thy words thou shalt be condemned." (Matthew 12:36-37)

8

Your Fifth Season: The Soul Winning Season

The fruit of the righteous is a tree of life; and he that winneth
souls is wise. Behold, the righteous shall be recompensed
in the earth: much more the wicked and the sinner.

(Proverbs 11:30-31)

I would be remiss if I did not use this opportunity to encourage or inspire you, the follower of Christ, to share the love of Jesus during this season. So many people are hurting emotionally, mentally, physically, and spiritually; and there's no better time than now for us, the believers, to demonstrate our love to them and witness to lost souls about the supreme love of God. As we reap a harvest of blessings in this season, let us remember the less fortunate souls. *"… therefore with lovingkindness have I drawn thee."* (Jeremiah 31:3b) Remember when we were lost in sin, someone witnessed to us about God's love and His salvation. And it was God the Father in heaven who drew us to Jesus Christ. For the words of Jesus reveal to us in John 6:44 that, *"No man can come to me, except the Father which hath sent me draw him: and I will raise him up at the last day."*

Apostle Paul also reminds us in Romans 5:6-8, *"For when we were yet without strength, in due time (at the right time) Christ died for the ungodly. For scarcely for a righteous man will one die: yet peradventure (perhaps) for a good man some would even dare to die. But God commendeth his (demonstrates his own) love towards us, in that, while we were yet sinners, Christ died for us."* John 3:16 reaffirms this verse, *"For God so loved the world, that he gave his only begotten Son, that whosoever believeth in him should not perish, but have everlasting life."*

My brothers and sisters, let us not be ashamed of our Lord and Savior, Jesus Christ, neither be selfish with our salvation in this season. Allow me to admonish you to share the love of Jesus during these perilous times with as many souls as possible, because Jesus is soon to come. I don't know about you, but I desire that my loved ones, whether rich, middle-class, or poor, be saved and have eternal life. *"For what shall it profit a man, if he shall gain the whole world, and lose his own soul? Whosoever therefore shall be ashamed of me and of my words in this adulterous and sinful generation; of him also shall the Son of man be ashamed, when he cometh in the glory of his Father with the holy angels."* (Mark 8:36-38)

Over two thousand years ago Jesus shed His blood on Calvary that we may be healed, delivered, and set free. Let us take advantage of this opportune time to elevate our communication with the world about the wondrous working power in the blood of Jesus. In 1876, the songwriter, Robert Lowry, penned the following words in verses one and three of this powerful song:

Nothing But the Blood

1) What can wash away my sin? Nothing but the blood of Jesus; What can make me whole again? Nothing but the blood of Jesus. (Chorus) O! precious is the flow that makes me white as snow; No other fount I know; Nothing but the blood of Jesus. 2) Nothing can for sin atone, Nothing but the blood of Jesus; Naught of good that I have done, Nothing but the blood of Jesus. (Chorus) O! precious is the flow that makes me white as snow; No other fount I know; Nothing but the blood of Jesus.

Hallelujah to the Lamb of God! *"…almost all things are puri-fied with blood, and without shedding of blood there is no remission."* (Hebrews 9:22) *"But he was wounded for our transgressions, he was bruised for our iniquities: the chastisement of our peace was upon him; and with his stripes we are healed.* (Isaiah 53:5)

Whether you are in your fifth season or not, God is calling for us to be fishers of men. (Read Matthew 4:18-22) Child of God, our ultimate goal should include reaching the lost at any cost and sharing the benefits of the joy we experience. During this perilous time, it is the ideal season for our loved ones, friends, and strangers alike to accept Jesus Christ as their personal savior before their life on earth deceases. And it could happen just because we took the time to share with them God's love and His salvation plan.

What about the backslider? Well, let us first see what a back-slider is. According to Wikipedia.com; Backsliding, also known as falling away or described as "committing apostasy," is a term used within Christianity to describe a process by which an individual who has converted to Christianity reverts to pre-conversion habits and/ or lapses or falls into sin; when a person turns from God to pursue their own desire. In the King James Version, the only time the word backslider is found is in Proverbs: *"The backslider in heart shall be filled with his own ways…"* (Proverbs 14:14).

Can a backslider be saved? Yes, just as the prodigal son came to himself and repented, and the father received him back with a hug, a kiss, and a feast, the same spirit of welcoming will take place with our heavenly father if today's backslider comes to his senses and repent. Our heavenly father will forgive him and gladly receive him unto himself. (Read Luke 15:11-32) David was also a backslider, who returned to God and asked Him for forgiveness, and God forgave him. Oh my, what a painful and miserable life and guilty feelings David must have experienced before coming to his senses. (Read Psalm 51). *"Restore unto me the joy of thy salvation; and uphold me with thy free (generous) spirit."* (Psalm 51:12)

Let us pray for the backsliders that they will come to themselves and repent before it is too late. "Backslider, God wants YOU back." If you do not repent, your soul will be lost. (Read Ezekiel 33:18) You must return to God and repent in order to be saved. *"Return, ye backsliding children, and I will heal your backslidings…"* (Jeremiah 3:22)

Wow! I honestly believe that I was compelled to add this chapter in my book. Regardless of how God is blessing us in our fifth season, if we are not witnessing and winning souls for Christ, we are not living to the full potential of our calling in Him. Children of God, our aspiration should be to live holy, share the love of Jesus, and be on a soul winning mission for the Lord. Remember, only what we do for Christ will last!

A Sinner's Prayer for Salvation

"That if thou shalt confess with thy mouth the Lord Jesus, and shalt believe in thine heart that God hath raised him from the dead, thou shalt be save. For with the heart man believeth unto righteousness; and with the mouth confession is made unto salvation." (Romans 10:9-10)

If you have not already accepted Jesus Christ as your personal savior, and asked Him to abide in your heart today, it is not too late. Do it today; for tomorrow is not promised. Today could be the first day of the beginning of the rest of your life as a born-again Christian. If you pray the following prayer with a sincere heart, you will be saved.

The Prayer

Dear Lord Jesus, I know that I am a sinner, and I confess my sins and ask for your forgiveness. I believe You died for my sins and rose from the dead. Please come into my heart as my Lord and Savior. Take complete control of my life and help me to walk in Your footsteps daily by the power of the Holy Spirit. Thank you, Lord for saving me. Amen.

If you prayed this prayer, you are certainly free. *"If the Son therefore shall make you free, ye shall be free indeed."* (John 8:36) It is done. *"Stand fast therefore in the liberty wherewith Christ hath made us free, and be not entangled again with the yoke of bondage."* (Galatians 5:1)

Child of God, have faith in God, and share with others the miracle of God's salvation, which is the greatest miracle. Continue to strive for a closer relationship with Him through reading God's Word, prayer, fasting, and maintaining fellowship with other Christian Believers. Do not be idle. Attend your church services faithfully, whether it is virtually or in person, and do not allow the enemy to persuade you to deviate or be entangled again with the yoke of bondage. Praise God! Spiritually speaking, this is truly your Fifth Season.

Praise the Lord, I'm Free

Your Fifth Season Benefits - Can You Name Them?

Now is the time to relax and have some fun. Listed below are Fifth Season phrases including one or more words, which are amid God's promises to us. The letters in each phrase are scrambled. Unscramble them by rearranging the letters to spell the answer word or phrase correctly. Each one is mentioned at least once in this book. The answers are located at the end of this exercise.

Example: CENBDANUA

Answer: ABUNDANCE

1. **LVWORFEO** _____

2. **CRIVYOT** _____

3. **ARELMIC** _____

4. **RHGTABEKOHUR** _____

5. **EVINECLDARE** _____

6. **ACEPE** _____

7. **ONIRTESARTO** _____

8. **CYORVERE** _____

9. **VATHSER** _____

10. **RATEGER** _____

11. **ESNRICEA** _____

12. **TRASELUPRANU ARFVO** _____

Answers:

1. OVERFLOW 2. VICTORY 3. MIRACLE 4. BREAKTHROUGH 5. DELIVERANCE 6. PEACE 7. RESTO-
RATION 8. RECOVERY 9. HARVEST 10. GREATER 11. INCREASE 12. SUPERNATURAL FAVOR

Great Is Thy Faithfulness

1923

Written by Thomas O. Chisholm

The music was composed by William M. Runyan

Great is Thy faithfulness, O God my Father,
There is no shadow of turning with Thee;

Thou changest not, Thy compassions they fail not;
As Thou hast been Thou forever wilt be.

Summer and winter And springtime and harvest,
Sun, moon, and stars in their courses above;

Join with all nature in manifold witness To Thy
great faithfulness, Mercy, and love.

Pardon for sin and a peace that endureth, Thine
own dear presence to cheer and to guide; Strength
for today and bright hope for tomorrow,

Blessings all mine, With ten thousand beside!

Great is Thy faithfulness.

'Tis So Sweet to Trust in Jesus

1882

Written by Louisa M. R. Stead
Composed by William J. Kirkpatrick

'Tis so sweet to trust in Jesus, Just to take Him at His word; Just to rest upon His promise; Just to know "Thus saith the Lord."

O how sweet to trust in Jesus, Just to trust His cleansing blood; Just in simple faith to plunge me, Neath the healing, cleansing flood!

Yes, 'tis sweet to trust in Jesus, Just from sin and self to cease; Just from Jesus simply taking, Life and rest and joy and peace.

I'm so glad I learned to trust Thee, Precious Jesus, Savior friend; And I know that Thou art with me, Wilt be with me to the end.

Chorus: Jesus, Jesus how I trust Him! How I've proved Him o'er and o'er! Jesus, Jesus, precious Jesus! O for grace to trust Him more.

Biblical Nuggets

This book of the law shall not depart out of thy mouth; but thou shalt meditate therein day and night, that thou mayest observe to do according to all that is written therein: for then thou shalt make thy way prosperous, and then thou shalt have good success. (Joshua 1:8) God's promise

Have not I commanded thee? Be strong and of a good courage; be not afraid, neither be thou dismayed: for the Lord thy God is with thee withersoever thou goest. (Joshua 1:9) God's promise

If my people, which are called by my name, shall humble themselves, and pray, and seek my face, and turn from their wicked ways; then will I hear from heaven, and will forgive their sin, and will heal their land. (2 Chronicles 7:14) God's promise

And said, Naked came I out of my mother's womb, and naked shall I return thither: the Lord gave, and the Lord hath taken away; blessed be the name of the Lord. In all this Job sinned not, nor charged God foolishly. (Job 1:21-22)

Behold, happy is the man whom God correcteth: therefore despise not the chastening of the Almighty. (Job 5:17)

If a man die, shall he live again? All the days of my appointed time will I wait, till my change come. (Job 14:14)

He that hath clean hands, and a pure heart; who hath not lifted up his soul into vanity, nor sworn deceitfully. He shall receive the blessing from the Lord, and righteousness from the God of his salvation. (Psalm 24:4-5) God's promise

Lift up your heads, O ye gates; and be ye lifted up, ye everlasting doors; and the King of glory shall come in. Who is this King of glory? The Lord strong and mighty, the Lord mighty in battle. (Psalm 24:7-8) God's promise

I had fainted, unless I had believed to see the goodness of the Lord in the land of the living. Wait on the Lord; be of good courage, and he shall strengthen thine heart: wait, I say, on the Lord. (Psalm 27:13-14) God's promise

For his anger endureth but a moment; in his favor is life: weeping may endure for a night, but joy cometh in the morning. (Psalm 30:5) God's promise

Rejoice in the Lord, O ye righteous: for praise is comely for the upright. (Psalm 33:1)

The steps of a good man are ordered by the Lord: and he delighteth in his way. (Psalm 37:23)

Mark the perfect man, and behold the upright: for the end of that man is peace. (Psalm 37:37) God's promise

If I were hungry, I would not tell thee: for the world is mine, and the fullness thereof. (Psalm 50:12)

Offer unto God thanksgiving; and pay thy vows into the Most High: And call upon me in the day of trouble: I will deliver thee, and thou shalt glorify me. (Psalm 50:14-15) God's promise

He sent his word, and healed them, and delivered them from their destructions. Oh that men would praise the Lord for his goodness, and for his wonderful works to the children of men! (Psalm 107:20-21)

Honor the Lord with thy substance, and with the first fruits of all thine increase: So shall thy barns be filled with plenty, and thy presses shall burst out with new wine. (Proverbs 3:9-10) God's promise

Wisdom is the principal thing; therefore get wisdom: and with all thy getting get understanding. (Proverbs 4:7)

Boast not thyself of tomorrow; for thou knowest not what a day may bring forth. Let another man praise thee, and not thine own mouth; a stranger, and not thine own lips. (Proverbs 27:1-2)

Come now, and let us reason together, saith the Lord: though your sins be as scarlet, they shall be as white as snow; though they be red like crimson, they shall be as wool. If ye be willing and obedient, ye shall eat the good of the land. (Isaiah 1:18-19) God's promise

For unto us a child is born, unto us a son is given: and the government shall be upon his shoulder: and his name shall be called Wonderful, Counselor, The might God, The everlasting Father, The Prince of Peace. (Isaiah 9:6)

Hast thou not known? Hast thou not heard that the everlasting God, the Lord, the Creator of the ends of the earth, fainteth not, neither is weary? There is no searching of his understanding. He giveth power to the faint; and to them that have no might he increaseth strength. (Isaiah 40:28-29)

To appoint unto them that mourn in Zion, to give unto them beauty for ashes, the oil of joy for mourning, the garment of praise for the spirit of heaviness; that they might be called trees of righteousness, the planting of the Lord, that he might me glorified. (Isaiah 61:3)

Come unto me, all ye that labor and are heavy laden, and I will give you rest. Take my yoke upon you, and learn of me; for I am meek and lowly in heart: and ye shall find rest unto your souls. For my yoke is easy, and my burden is light. (Matthew 11:28-30) God's promise

Jesus answered and said unto them, Verily I say unto you, If ye have faith, and doubt not, ye shall not only do this which is done to the fig tree, but also if ye shall say unto this mountain, Be thou removed, and be thou cast into the sea; it shall be done. And all things, whatsoever ye shall ask in prayer, believing, ye shall receive. (Matthew 21:21-22) God's promise.

Go ye therefore, and teach all nations, baptizing them in the name of the Father, and of the son, and of the Holy Ghost: Teaching them to observe all things whatsoever I have commanded you: and, lo, I am with you always, even unto the end of the world. Amen. (Matthew 28:19-20) God's promise

For God so loved the world, that he gave his only begotten Son, that whosoever believeth in him should not perish, but have everlasting life. (John 3:16) God's promise

But as it is written, Eye hath not seen, nor ear heard, neither have entered into the heart of man, the things which God hath prepared for them that love him. (1 Corinthians 2:9) God's promise

Finally, brethren, whatsoever things are true, whatsoever things are honest, whatsoever things are just, whatsoever things are pure, whatsoever things are lovely, whatsoever things are of good report; if there be any virtue, and if there be any praise, think on these things. (Philippians 4:8)

Sources Cited

Nelson (1988). *King James Study Bible.* Nashville, TN: Thomas Nelson Publishers

Nelson (2005). *King James Version.*

Nashville TN: Thomas Nelson Publishers

Robert J. Morgan (2011). *Then Sings My Soul.*

Nashville, TN: W Publishing Group

Marcus Gentry. 101 Ponderables To Initiate Conversation Above and Beyond

https://www.britannica.com

https://Wikipedia.com

My Notes

My Notes

The Author's Contact Information

For Speaking engagements or to place an order, please contact:

Lottie N. Pitts

P. O. Box 952 Matteson, Illinois 60443

Email addresses: lottiesgifts1@sbcglobal.net

pittslottie51@icloud.com

Websites:

lottiepitts.ueniweb.com

lottiepitts.net

Dr. Pitts' other literary works that are available:

Overcoming Your Fear and Other Issues With Your Faith and Works - Outskirts Press, Publisher

In this book you will discover how to receive God's deliverance and live an overcoming victorious and liberated life from the spirit of fear and other hindrances that come to block your breakthrough. It is filled with Biblical principles that will set you free and break every chain that is holding you hostage. You are an overcomer. $13.95

Love Word Search Puzzles & Bible Trivia

A fun and wholesome way to occupy your time. It is a stress reliever with unique word search puzzles, Bible trivia, and inspirational words that could be just what you need for such a time as this. Answers included. $5.99

Shipping & Handling - $2.95

Please allow 1-2 weeks for delivery.

A Brief Bio and Photo of the Author and her husband, Thaddeus.

D r. Pitts is an evangelist, pastor's wife, motivational speaker, retired schoolteacher, former reading and math tutor, author, former editor and publisher of her own Christian magazines, and retired Owner/Director of T.H.E. Learning Center, Chicago, Illinois. For several years, she served as the Senior Editor of the Holiness Today Magazine for the C. H. Mason International Historical Society, C.O.G.I.C., Inc.

Dr. Pitts is a lifelong member of the Church of God in Christ. She received her calling as a missionary at the tender age of eighteen years old. She has been a faithful servant in the Northern Illinois Jurisdiction, Church Of God In Christ for over fifty years, and a licensed evangelist for over thirty-five years. She has conducted revivals and been the Guest Speaker on various occasions including Annual Women's Day Services and Conferences. Among other prominent positions, she served as a District Missionary in the Dr.

T.R. Jackson District for 25 years and as the President of the District Pastors and Ministers' Wives Alliance for seven years. Presently, she serves as an Assistant State Supervisor with the Northern Illinois Jurisdiction, C.O.G.I.C., Department of Women and a member of the NIJ Leadership Development.

Dr. Pitts is known for her powerful and inspirational messages intreating her audiences to live a holy and victorious life in Christ Jesus. She has worked faithfully by her husband, Elder Dr. Thaddeus L. Pitts, who has served for twenty-two years as the pastor of Greater Jackson Tabernacle Church Of God In Christ of Chicago, Illinois. She and her husband have two fine sons and daughters in love, and four wonderful grandchildren. Some of her favorite scriptures are Psalm 34:1-3, 19, Galatians 6:9, and Ephesians 3:20.

YOUR FIFTH SEASON

Expect It to Happen Again and Again!

Now unto him that is able to do exceeding abundantly above all that we ask or think, according to the power that worketh in us. Unto him be glory in the church by Christ Jesus throughout all ages, world with out end. Amen. (Ephesians 3:20-21)

To God be the Glory for the Things He has Done.

I will extol (praise) thee, my God, O king; and I will bless thy name for ever and ever. Every day will I bless thee; and I will praise thy name for ever and ever. Great is the Lord, and greatly to be praised; and his greatness is unsearchable. One generation shall praise thy works to another, and shall declare thy mighty acts. I will speak of the glorious honor of thy majesty, and of thy wondrous works. (Psalm 145:1-5)

CPSIA information can be obtained
at www.ICGtesting.com
Printed in the USA
BVHW040453120422
633739BV00006B/84